The Forbidden City: The History of the Chinese Imperial Palace of the Ming and Qing Dynasties in Beijing

By Charles River Editors

A picture of the East Glorious Gate

About Charles River Editors

Charles River Editors is a boutique digital publishing company, specializing in bringing history back to life with educational and engaging books on a wide range of topics. Keep up to date with our new and free offerings with this 5 second sign up on our weekly mailing list, and visit Our Kindle Author Page to see other recently published Kindle titles.

We make these books for you and always want to know our readers' opinions, so we encourage you to leave reviews and look forward to publishing new and exciting titles each week.

Introduction

A picture of the Shenwumen Gate

The Forbidden City

Located in the center of Beijing, the Forbidden City served as the palace for the emperor of China from 1420 to 1912 CE, a period encompassing the Ming and Qing dynasties. It was home to the celestial leaders of China, men that possessed the Mandate of Heaven. A total of 24 emperors lived and ruled from the vast and magnificent complex for almost 500 years, until the last Chinese dynasty was overthrown in 1912 with the abdication of Emperor Xuantong, more commonly known as Puyi.

Known also as the Forbidden Palace, or amongst contemporary Chinese as the "Former Palace," the complex was first given its name in 1576. The Forbidden City was the home of many thousands of governmental staff, female servants and concubines, eunuchs, soldiers, and kitchen staff, and where their entire lives were built. Nonetheless, entrance to it from the outside was forbidden to all but the emperor, his court, and his relations.

Without the permission of the emperor, access to or from the heart of the empire was impossible, but what was once inaccessible is now one of the most visited institutions in the world. Today, the Forbidden City is a UNESCO World Heritage site, operated as the largest museum in the world and located in the heart of the capital of the world's most populous country.

The Forbidden City: The History of the Chinese Imperial Palace of the Ming and Qing Dynasties in Beijing examines the history of the palace. Along with pictures of important people, places, and events, you will learn about the Forbidden City like never before.

The Forbidden City: The History of the Chinese Imperial Palace of the Ming and Qing Dynasties in Beijing

About Charles River Editors

Introduction

   Chapter 1: The Historical and Urban Context

   Chapter 2: Structures and Spaces

   Chapter 3: Residents and Staff

   Chapter 4: Interiors and Activities

   Chapter 5: The Forbidden City in Modern Chinese History

   Chapter 6: Conclusion

   Online Resources

   Bibliography

Free Books by Charles River Editors

Discounted Books by Charles River Editors

Chapter 1: The Historical and Urban Context

China's capital has changed location frequently throughout history. The former Han Dynasty had its capital at Chang'an, and the Eastern Han Dynasty at Luoyang. For most subsequent dynasties, Chang'an was the heart of Chinese civilization, with the eastern capital of Luoyang to the east as a second center. Jiankang (modern Nanjing) later became the new capital in the south in 316, under the Eastern Jin Dynasty (316-420 CE). By 1050 CE, under the Song Dynasty, Kaifeng had become the imperial capital.

Beijing was only first considered a capital under the Great Jin dynasty (1115-1234 CE). In 1151, under the instruction of Emperor Wanyan Liang, the imperial capital was moved from Huining in the Shangjing region of Manchuria, to Yanjing (modern Beijing). Under Zhenyuan, the next emperor, many developments were made in the city, the name of which was changed to Zhongdu ("Central Capital").

Significant developments took place under the Yuan (1271-1368 CE), a dynasty founded by the invading Mongols, led by Khublai Khan. In 1265 CE, the Khan commissioned Muslim architects to design and construct a carefully planned imperial palace-city in Tatu, north of present day Beijing. Their palace incorporated a fusion of Chinese and Mongol styles, and a symmetrical ground plan which followed a cardinal axis. It was destroyed when the Mongols were expelled from China in 1368, but memories of the classically planned administrative city, with its regular streets and great enclosing walls, lingered.

The Ming (1368-1644 CE) replaced the Yuan dynasty. Their focus was to restore ethnic Chinese rule and culture over the country, following the Mongol hegemony of the Yuan. They were patrons to a large number of architects, engineers, and artisans, and renewed agricultural and commercial growth, with policies controlled by an efficient, centralized bureaucracy. Under the Ming, the country's population boomed to the highest of any country in the world at that time. However, this was also the beginning of China's isolation. During this time, foreign merchants were closely supervised by the imperial armies, and restricted to a limited number of ports. Chinese traders were not allowed to trade overseas, and during this time, the large shipyards of the Yuan were closed. The Ming continued to be assaulted by Mongol armies from the north and the west, and during this time, the Great Wall of China was further fortified.

Although they initially located their capital at Nanjing, in 1406, Emperor Yongle (r. 1403-1424) announced it would be moved north to Yanjiang. Construction of the new imperial complex began the following year, close to the location of the Yuan palace, and in a similar style. The name of the city was changed to Beijing ("Northern Capital") after the Forbidden City was completed in 1420, and from that point onwards, the ceremonial and administrative governance of the country was focused on Beijing. Emperors of the Ming dynasty came from the house of Zhu, fourteen of which occupied the Forbidden City between 1420 and 1644. Heirs to the throne were often chosen at a young age, whilst his brothers were sent away from the palace to homes outside of Beijing.

The Yongle Emperor

The Ming emperors made themselves the direct rulers of the realm, rather than using chief ministers as the Mongols had. They reinstated the Confucian civil service examination system to restore a traditionally meritocratic government. Mandarins, or official imperial emissaries, were sent to each of the provinces to ensure that the emperor's orders were carried out, and to border regions to demand that they recognize their subordination to the Son of Heaven. The strength of the dynasty was further supported by the introduction of eunuchs to the Forbidden City staff.

A Ming dynasty depiction of the palace

The Ming was the last native (i.e., Han) dynasty in China. A great factor in the decline of the dynasty was the growing power of the Manchus to China's northeast. In April, 1644, a rebel leader from Hubei called Li Zi Cheng invaded the Forbidden City. His armies defeated the imperial guards, and after a series of sieges, had broken through into the inner courts. As the invading forces streamed through the Wumen Gate, the last Ming emperor committed suicide by hanging himself on a hill behind the palace. Li Zi Cheng declared himself emperor of the Shun dynasty, however, his rule was short-lived.

The Ming general, Wu Sangui, formed a coalition between the remaining Ming soldiers and those of Manchuria. The combined forces overwhelmed the Shun armies, and a few weeks after the coronation of Li Zi Cheng, a tremendous force of Mongol and Manchu soldiers marched upon the imperial capital. A young child from the Aisin Gioro family, named Fu Lin who was only five years old, was established as Emperor Shunzhi, first of the Qing dynasty (1644-1912). Large parts of Beijing and the Forbidden City were burned in the ensuing destruction, but the city quickly recovered and developed into one of the most splendid centers of culture and governance in the country.

Manchu cultural hegemony spread across China's north through their military might, and they developed a strict governmental framework to control the Han majority of the population. They made a number of social and economic reforms, reorganizing the country's system of taxation, expanding the bureaucracy (which, in turn, became infamously corrupt), and adopting Neo-Confucian values that emphasized the role of the patriarchy.

Altogether, ten emperors from the Aisin Gioro family occupied the Forbidden City. Unlike the Ming, under the Qing, all sons of the emperor were considered eligible heirs and kept within the confines of the Forbidden City's walls. Regardless of whether they became emperor or not, all were educated in governmental affairs, and after evaluation, given positions in the management of the empire, based on their merits.

The Han Chinese resisted their new Manchu rulers, in particular, as they opened China up to exploitation from the West during the nineteenth century. A continued boom in the population, which grew to more than three hundred million people, brought increasing needs for resources and modernizing reforms, however, the Qing refusal to address the needs of their subjects eventually led to the downfall of the dynasty, and of the three thousand year old imperial system.

For almost five centuries, the Forbidden City was the beating heart of Chinese governance at the center of Beijing. The imperial palace complex was one of four interconnected cities that, together, created the capital. It was surrounded by three carefully planned and walled districts. The holistic symmetry and geometric design of the overall urban landscape is extraordinary: a central axis is created by the Forbidden City, which is oriented according to the cardinal directions. The Imperial Way extends to its south, a well-maintained road of flagstones extending north to south through Beijing, that only the emperor could use (there were some exceptions–on the day of their wedding, the empress could travel with her husband along the Imperial Way, and after passing the stringent Confucian examination system, graduating students formed a procession down the royal road). The formality and symmetry of the city promoted the power of the imperial family, though some believe that the entire city is oriented towards Xanadu, the summer capital of the Yuan dynasty (the ruins of which are located in modern-day Inner Mongolia).

Surrounding the Forbidden City was the Imperial City. This area was surrounded by a formidable wall, almost two meters thick, four and a half meters high, and thirteen miles in circumference. Three lakes were located within this area: the Beihai, Zhonghai, and Nanhai.

Around these were built a number of temples and pavilions for the relaxation of the elite. A great number of Buddhist temples and shrines testify to the importance these held for elite Chinese society at this time. Tibetan denominations were particularly revered during the Qing dynasty, as seen in the White Pagoda Temple built in 1651, in honor of the visiting Dalai Lama. Others include the Mahakala and Fayuansi temples, the latter of which was used by lamas from Mongolia to produce Tibetan Buddhist manuscripts. There was even a Catholic church. Many significant Confucian sites were also located within the Imperial City, such as the Tai Miao ("Temple of the Imperial Ancestors"), where sacrifices and other ceremonies were held in honor of imperial ancestors during both the Ming and Qing dynasties. There were also the imperial stables, warehouses, workshops, and the Imperial Household Department, which managed accommodation requirements of the guests and residents of the Inner City.

Surrounding the Imperial City was the Inner City, approximately twenty five miles in circumference. It served as the administrative center of the Qing, overseen by the Imperial Household Department, and contained many important governing institutions, such as the office of the Censor-in-chief, the highest-ranking state official of the empire. Administration of the imperial armies was carried out there, and approximately one hundred and thirty thousand banner men resided in the Inner City. Other residents came from diverse parts of the region: Han Chinese awarded the privilege by the grace of the Emperor, Russians captured from the Albazin conquests in 1685, a group of Russian orthodox priests that arrived in 1727, proselytizing Europeans, Tibetans, and Uyghur Muslim elites and craftsmen from the Western Regions (present-day Xinjiang region).

Extending from the southern wall of the Inner City was the Outer City, a warren of siheyuan neighborhoods and hutong streets. This was the center of commerce in the capital. In the streets surrounding the access points between the Inner and Outer cities–the Xuanwu, Zhengyang, and Chongwen gates–were bustling shopping districts, containing several hundred shops. The Outer City also contained a thriving brothel district, which were frequented by the soldiers of the imperial army.

To the west, north, and east of the Forbidden City were magnificent imperial gardens, such as Jingshan, also known as "Prospect Hill," a manmade hill created when the Palace Moat was excavated. West of the Forbidden City is the Zhongnanhai imperial garden, which today serves as the location of the Chinese Communist Party headquarters. Further west and to the north is the Beihai Park, which dates from the eleventh century, and is one of the largest imperial gardens in the country.

Chapter 2: Structures and Spaces

The Forbidden Palace from Jingshan Park

The structural form of the Forbidden City is inextricably part of its heritage value. The stories of those that ruled China would not be the same without the uniquely vast and magnificent complex of residences, halls, palaces, walls, and gates. The Forbidden City is rectangular in form. North to south it measures approximately nine hundred and sixty meters, and east to west it is approximately seven hundred and fifty meters, creating an enclosed area of about one hundred and eighty acres. This enclosed space contains around nine hundred and eighty buildings.

Construction of the Forbidden City took fourteen years, between 1406 and 1420. More than one million laborers were employed or enslaved to work on the site. The massive walls were made of rammed earth, faced with numerous layers of baked brick and mortar. The buildings are almost all made of timber, which was mostly imported from the tropical southern Chinese provinces. Locally quarried marble was also used throughout the complex. The famous kilns of Suzhou (in today's Jiangsu province) produced "golden bricks" with which the floors of many interiors in the complex were paved.

The passage of time has revealed much new information on the skills of those that originally constructed the Forbidden City. For example, it was only in the twentieth century, after centuries of weathering, that the ingenuity of the stone carvers employed to create the bas-relief ramps leading to the Zhonghe Hall was revealed. Some of the largest blocks of stone used in the Forbidden City weighed between two and three hundred tons, and had to be transported for more than seventy kilometers from the quarries at which they were sourced. Recent research has shown that these rocks were transported over this great distance by being slid along roads of ice. Furthermore, the ramps of the Forbidden City were believed to have been created out of single slabs of stone, but recent research has revealed that the seam was cleverly disguised by master stone carvers.

    The management of space and access is linked to power and social hierarchy. The ground plan of the Forbidden City exemplified the relationship between both physical and intangible boundaries and socio-political status. The Forbidden City's boundaries were set by an eight meter high and almost nine meter thick retaining wall, and a moat that was eight meters deep and over fifty meters wide. Situated at each corner of the rectangular walls were towers with ridged roofs. Four gates provided access to and from the confines within. Movement between the gates was strictly controlled, and the vast amount of governmental staff and foreign dignitaries would never have been given access through even the outer gates.

Charlie Fong's picture of the northwestern corner tower

Imperial roof decoration of the highest status on the roof ridge of the Hall of Supreme

Harmony

Access to the Imperial City from the south was via the iconic Tiananmen ("Heavenly Peace) Gate–a massive, fortified tower with five round-arched gateways. Only the emperor could make use of the central gateway. Visitors would pass those on either side, and then through the Duanman Gate, otherwise known as the "Upright Gate," before eventually crossing the Palace Moat, and coming upon the Forbidden City.

From the Duanman Gate, the Imperial Way passed through the southern Wumen Gate, known today as the Meridian Gate. This gate extends south on either side of the Imperial Way in a U-shaped enclosure. Access through the gate was by one of the five smaller gateways set into its base. Visitors would experience a sense of great awe by the contrasting size of the high walls on all sides. The small doorways would have been accentuated by the presence of imperial elephants, which would have stood in between each of the five small gateways. Altogether, these would have made the visitor feel quite diminutive, however, the Wumen Gate was rarely used by anyone other than the emperor, and remained closed for most of the year (the one exception occurred following the examinations for positions to work in the palace, when the top three scorers were allowed to walk through the privileged gateway).

Leonard G.'s picture of the Meridian Gate

Most access was through the eastern, western, and northern gates. To the east was the Donghua (Glorious East) Gate, through which civil officials would pass. To the west was the Xihua (Glorious West) Gate, through which military officials would pass. To the north was the Shenwu ("Spiritual Valor") Gate. This provided access to the imperial gardens at Jingshan. It was mostly the imperial consorts that made use of this gate.

The high walls and impenetrable gates of the Forbidden City effectively kept the common people out, and the imperial family within. The safety of the ruling family's lineage was of paramount importance–a male heir had to be ensured in order to continue the dynasty. Therefore, great measures were taken to prevent any risk to the safety of the emperor and his family.

Furthermore, by preventing any unauthorized access and hiring only females and castrated eunuchs as staff, it was assured that the emperor could be the only father of children born within the palace walls. Access to the Forbidden City was tightly controlled, both by day and by night. After dark, the only way into the palace was with a specially designed pair of matching blocks, inscribed with the characters "Sagely Edict," which could only be received by order of the emperor. The gates were sealed by massive locked doors, each embellished by a grid of golden nails. The walls had defensive functions, manned with imperial guards that ensured no one infiltrated or escaped from the city. Moreover, the formidable size of these walls, their striking vermillion color, and their towers would have been visible far and wide across Beijing. The visitor's feeling of awe passing through the gates leading from the outer areas of Beijing to the inner sanctum of the empire would have been accentuated by the progressively monumental architecture surrounding them.

The Forbidden City can be divided into two sections–the Outer Court to the south, also known as the Front Court, and the Inner Court to the north, also known as the Back Palace. Although his feet would not have touched the ground, it would have taken the eight to sixteen eunuchs roughly one and a half hours to carry the emperor on a sedan chair from the southernmost to the northernmost part of the Forbidden City.

The Outer Court consists of the southern and lowest part of the complex, and was where most of the significant ceremonial structures were located, and the public ritual activities took place. As one enters through the Wumen Gate the Imperial Way crosses over one of the five bridges that pass over the flowing waters of the Inner Golden River. Another gate follows–the Gate of Supreme Harmony, flanked to the west by the Zhendu Gate and to the East by the Zhaode Gate. This provides access to a massive open square, the Waichao ("Outer Court"), with the Taihe ("Supreme Harmony"), Zhonghe ("Central Harmony"), and Baohe ("Preserving Harmony") Halls rising on a marble platform of three tiers from its northern edge. To the west is the Hongyi Pavilion, and to the East is the Tiren Pavilion.

The Gate of Supreme Harmony

Daniel Case's picture of the Hall of Supreme Harmony

The throne in the Hall of Preserving Harmony

These three central halls are the central point of the Forbidden City, and were of prime importance for its residents and the population of China. The Taihe Hall was largest of the three in size, at over thirty meters tall. It was of great importance, serving as the ceremonial core of the city, where many important state rituals took place during the Ming, and to a lesser extent during the Qing. The Qing Emperor performed annual ploughing rites here to ensure a good harvest for the country, and it was in the Taihe Hall that he prepared for this ceremony by closely inspecting the tools. This is the largest ancient timber structure in China. Within is housed the splendid "Xuanyuan Mirror," a glass and mercury ball representing the emperor, held within the mouth of a dragon suspended on the roof. The Zhonghe Hall is slightly smaller than the Taihe. This square-shaped structure was also used to prepare for imperial ceremonies. Finally, the Baohe Hall was a space used to meet dignitaries from China's vassals. It was also the place where the last stage of the stringent state-wide examinations took place, and eventually where those that passed would receive their degrees.

Access to the three halls was by ramps leading from the ground level up the three terraces. Those at the center of the route of the Imperial Way were ornately decorated with bas-relief symbols of dragons. The largest bas-relief carving on a single stone block in China can be found on the ramp leading to the Baohe Hall. This massive rock, three meters by almost two meters, weighs more than two hundred tons. The Taihe Hall and Outer Court were ceremonial and administrative spaces, where the emperor would sit upon his elevated throne high above his supplicant civil and military servants.

Some important governmental departments were located within the confines of the Forbidden City. The civil Cabinet Hall was located within the Outer Court, just east of the Wumen Gate, and its military counterpart was located close to the western access point of the Inner Court. Southwest through the Hongyi Pavilion was the Hall of Military Prowess, which was built by Ming Emperor Yongle, to be occasionally used for meetings with his court. It later became the Forbidden City's official publishing house. Nearby was the Nanxun Hall, where some of the finest Confucian academics in the country gave lectures, and later where the Grand Secretariat had his offices. Other institutions included barracks of the imperial guard, and the Fanshufang, where a large staff of Manchu and Mandarin translators worked.

To the north of the three central audience halls and on an elevated area is the Inner Court. This was the most secluded and private part of the Forbidden City, accessed by two gates north of the Baohe Hall--the Jingyun Gate to the east and the Longzong Gate to the west. Few governmental services were located in the Inner Court, as it was here that the emperor resided, his family lived, and a vast staff of eunuchs and female servants operated. During the Ming period, this part of the Forbidden City was purely residential, but it gradually played a more important governmental role under the Qing, and in particular, during the reign of Emperor Kangxi (r. 1662-1722), who sought to distance himself from Han Chinese bureaucrats.

The Kangxi Emperor returning to the Forbidden City after a tour to the south

In the center of the Inner Court were two residential buildings, one each for the emperor and the empress. The Qianquin ("Heavenly Purity") Palace is situated symmetrically north of the terrace, upon which the Baohe Hall is located. It is accessed from the courtyard via the Qianquin Gate. This served as the official residence of the emperor, though under the Qing, it became increasingly used for business purposes. From the 1720s under the instructions of Emperor Yongzheng, the emperors resided in the nearby Palace of the Culture of the Mind. From that time onwards, the Qianquin Palace was used as a reception hall for the emperor and his advisors and visitors. It was at the Palace of the Culture of the Mind that empress dowager Cixi held meetings with her council and other governmental advisors during the final decades of the Qing dynasty.

The Palace of Heavenly Purity

The Palace of Earthly Tranquility is located further north. It was a nine by three bay large building, where the empress resided. The third building in this complex was the Jiao Tai Dian ("Hall of Union"), a square building that served as the official meeting place of the imperial couple, accessed by a cloistered hallway from their respective residences. Starting with the reign of Emperor Kangxi, this was also where the imperial seals were stored. These thirty-nine seals (reduced to twenty-five in 1746 under the orders of Emperor Qianlong) were the emperor's symbol of legitimacy and power. Written in both Mandarin and Manchu scripts and made of gold, jade and sandalwood, he used them to make and stamp official imperial orders.

Behind the imperial residences was the Imperial Garden, containing the Hall of Clocks and Watches, and Qin'an ("Imperial Peace") Hall. On the northern edge of the garden is the Shenwu ("Spiritual Valor") Gate, the northern exit from the Forbidden City. To the east of the Imperial Garden was the Qian Dong Wu Suo, five residential compounds where Emperor Daoguang's (r. 1821-1850) children lived. Smaller gateways on either side of the Qianqing gate led to the east and west of the central area, where two roughly symmetrical groups of six palaces were located. In 1420, Emperor Qianlong had the Palace of Eternal Longevity added to the Six Western Palace complex, to be used as a residence for the empress, empress dowager, imperial children and grandchildren, consorts, eunuchs, and maids. To the south of the Western Palace complex was the emperor's alternative residence, occasionally also used to hold court with his ministers. Unlike the rest of the Forbidden City, this was quite a domestic sphere, without all of the architectural grandeur and promotion of power.

Few visitors passed the courtyard in front of the Qianquin Gate. They were, instead, met there by an intermediary, the Chancery of Memorials, who received gifts on behalf of the emperor, and who orally transmitted imperial messages coming from within the Inner Court. It was only through a tally provided by the chancery that visitors or officials would be able to attend an audience with their ruler.

Chapter 3: Residents and Staff

Who lived in the Forbidden City, and who had access from the outside? The court politics of the imperial palace are fascinating, filled with intrigue, backroom deals between people, competition to gain advantage, and sometimes situations that were downright bloody.

A succession of twenty-four rulers each made the Forbidden City their home from the fifteenth century until the early twentieth century.

Name	Reign
Ming Dynasty (1368–1644)	
Emperor Yongle	1403–1424
Emperor Hongxi	1425
Emperor Xuande	1426–1435
Emperor Zhengtong	1436–1449
Emperor Jingtai	1450–1456
Emperor Tianshun	1457–1464
Emperor Chenghua	1465–1487
Emperor Hongzhi	1488–1505
Emperor Zhengde	1506–1521
Emperor Jiajing	1522–1566
Emperor Longqing	1567–1572

Emperor Wanli   1573–1620

Emperor Taichang   1620

Emperor Tianqi   1621–1627

Emperor Chongzhen   1628–1644

Qing Dynasty (1644-1912)

Emperor Shunzhi   1644–1661

Emperor Kangxi   1662–1722

Emperor Yongzheng   1723–1735

Emperor Qianlong   1736–1795

Emperor Jiaqing   1796–1820

Emperor Daoguang   1821–1850

Emperor Xianfeng   1851–1861

Emperor Tongzhi   1862–1874

Emperor Guangxu   1875–1908

Emperor Xuantong (Puyi)   1909–1911

The emperor was also known as the "Son of Heaven," through his possession of tianming (the "Mandate of Heaven"). The Mandate of Heaven was the divine power believed to legitimize the rule of the emperor and dynasty. A number of signs and anomalies signaled that the emperor possessed the Mandate of Heaven, or otherwise portended the movement of tianming from one emperor to another. Certain inauspicious signs and events–such as floods, thunderstorms, drought, and famine–would indicate that the deities disapproved of the current emperor, and that he had lost the Mandate of Heaven.

Despite the homogeneity of the architectural landscape and regular ceremonies and rituals, each dynasty and emperor led a different way of life within the Forbidden City. Whilst most Ming rulers made Beijing their permanent residence, those of the Qing only stayed in the Forbidden City during particular seasons of the year. They would frequently escape outside of the city, or to villas and palaces elsewhere in the empire, such as Chengde and Mulan near the Great Wall of China. In addition, the Qing rulers made a number of modifications to the

Forbidden City. They changed the functions and names of many buildings, and moved a number of governmental functions deeper into the Inner Court.

Perhaps the most renowned generation of emperors existed following the death of the first Qing ruler, Shunzhi, who perished from smallpox in 1661, aged only twenty two. The emperors Kangxi, Yongzheng, and Qianlong, laid the solid foundations of the lengthy Qing dynasty, and are considered amongst the greatest to have existed in Chinese history. Emperor Kangxi was the longest reigning emperor, having sat on the imperial throne for more than sixty one years. Emperor Yongzheng was an incredibly effective and hardworking leader, whose motto was: "To be ruler is tough." He instituted many reliable financial and military policies that settled the dynasty's wealth and borders. His son, Emperor Qianlong, was famed for his cultural pursuits-- he was a skilled poet and calligrapher, patron of the arts, and collector of curios and antiquities. Furthermore, he was a triumphant military leader, establishing China's borders to roughly that of the modern nation. Qianlong's respect for his ancestors was so great, that in 1795, he chose to retire from the imperial throne after reigning for sixty years, not wishing to break the record set by Emperor Kangxi.

The Forbidden City was built to be the home of the emperor and his extensive family, a place where the safety of the dynastic lineage could be maintained by ensuring that no other males would be the fathers of the imperial heirs, and that no threats came from outside the palace walls. Nevertheless, despite the tall towers, imposing walls, and well-trained royal guard, a number of infiltrations occurred during the Ming and Qing. Some were put down quickly, such as the assassination attempt in 1803 by a man named Chen De, and the uprising in 1813 led by Lin Qing. Others, however, affected the entire empire, such as Li Zi Cheng's rebellion in 1644, which brought down the Ming dynasty.

The lives of the emperors were surrounded by symbolism and ritual. Certain symbols were repeated in the decorative scheme of the structures, clothing, art, furnishings, and objects of the imperial household. There are hundreds of symbols found in the Forbidden City: plants and fruits, real and mythical animals, abstract patterns, and auspicious characters. Some were associated solely with the Forbidden City and the life of the imperial household, whilst others were commonly found across China.

The ground plan, and architectural style of the Forbidden City, were built to promote the cosmological importance of Chinese traditional values. The entire city was planned from the beginning to be a miniaturized and harmonious representation of a well-ordered universe, according to Chinese cosmological belief. The juxtaposition of buildings with one another, such as the position of ancestral tombs before palaces, also reflected traditional Chinese values of social hierarchy and filial piety. The source of these traditions was the Classic of Rites, one of the most important Confucian texts. Purely traditional, and without external influences, the architecture of the site is believed to epitomize the timelessness of China's Confucian past.

Colors played a special role in the decorative style of the Forbidden City, and in the emperor's life. Yellow was the most widely used color, being associated solely with the power of the imperial family. Most of the tile roofs of the emperor's residential buildings are glazed in bright yellow. The color green was used in the tiles of the emperor's heir, as the color was believed to promote growth. Black tiles were used on the roof of the Pavilion of Literary Profundity, because the color was associated with water, and was thus believed to help prevent fires.

Numbers have great significance in the city. The number three is widely used across the complex, for example, in the cluster of halls found in the Inner and Outer Courts. In Chinese characters, the number three is represented by three straight and parallel horizontal lines–a symbol that also bears Daoist connotations, representing the auspicious Qian or "Heaven" trigram. Many structures also make use of the numbers six, five, and nine in their architectural form, being symbolically significant numbers in cosmological beliefs associated with the imperial family. For example, the Taihe Hall consists of nine bays west to east, and five bays north to south. A quick trick used to identify which buildings were most important was to count the number of statuettes used to embellish the sloping roof ridges. The greater the number of statuettes on the roof, the higher status of the building. For example, the Taihe Hall is a uniquely important space that features a record ten statuettes on each ridge.

One particular way in which the power of the emperor and social status of everybody else, was signified was through clothing that bore symbolically meaningful features. Rather than reflecting the emperor's personal taste, his wardrobe was carefully planned for the entire year in advance. Similarly, complex dress codes existed for everybody else involved in the Forbidden City. These laws controlled the shape, color, and fabric of clothing, the accessories, jewelry, and hats that could be worn, and the symbolic decoration that could be added, all according to the individual's rank and gender. The dress scheme changed frequently, according to the different seasons or particular events, and according to the level of formality required.

The dress code of the emperor changed between the Ming and Qing, though the careful advance planning of the wardrobe did not. Whereas the Ming style featured flowing robes, dainty slippers, and wearing one's hair long, the leaders of the Qing preferred clothing from their Manchurian homeland. They wore boots, trousers, and coats, reminiscent of their martial nomadic brethren. Furthermore, upon assuming control of the country, the Manchu court ordered the Han majority of the population to adopt the Manchu style of shaving one's head into a "queue" style, with a long ponytail. Both men and women wore traditional Manchu jackets, known as magua, over their robes, made from the most expensive, embroidered silk textiles available in the capital.

One particularly important symbol was that of the five-toed dragon, a creature that had been associated with the imperial family since the Song dynasty (960-1279 CE). More than twelve thousand dragons were incorporated into the decorative scheme of the structures in the

Forbidden City. One particularly fine dragon is seen in the Qianquin Palace, a coiled statue that is suspended from the roof above the imperial throne. They were believed to signify the relationship between good and evil in the world, and to portent great destruction through a number of astonishing natural phenomena (such as earthquakes, tornadoes, and waterspouts). Only the emperor was believed able to tame the dragons, thanks to Heaven's Mandate, which was the reason dragons were on the clothing worn only by the emperor, his family, and his consorts. Anyone else in the city or country found wearing dragons on their clothing would be executed (one way people got around this was by wearing images of four-toed dragons, which were not considered "real" dragons).

Indeed, the emperor was forced to wear clothing bearing dragon symbols, to eat his food off of dishes bearing dragon designs, and sleep in rooms decorated with even more dragon motifs. Just as no-one else could wear dragons on their clothing, the emperor could wear nothing but dragons; any desire to wear a robe that displayed a peacock, panda, or pig would have been impossible.

The Forbidden City was also home to the empress, empress dowager, consorts, concubines, and hundreds of female servants whose histories are all but forgotten. Their lives provide an alternative perspective into the Forbidden City. Not only was it forbidden for people to enter the sacred space, but for those living within its walls, there was rare opportunity to leave the cloistered environment. These women were mostly sequestered deep inside the Inner Court of the Forbidden City, and though they lived luxurious lives, they rarely had any contact with the outside world. The limited number that were able to leave the confines of the palace did so candidly, through the northernmost Shenwu Gate.

Little is known about the lives of non-elite women that resided in the Forbidden City. Female servants are mostly mentioned when they became chosen as concubines and consorts for the emperor. For the large part, they lived silent lives, invisibly serving the emperor from the background, and occasionally in an intimate capacity. The sole role of the concubines was to bear children for the emperor, to produce a male heir that will continue the dynastic lineage, in particular. Those that did give birth to sons became elevated to the position of imperial consort.

Some women wielded significant power within the palace, and even the nation. The power of the empress was greatly increased if she outlived her husband, at which point the widow would become an "empress dowager." Some empress dowagers kept hold of this power for extensive periods, by controlling the selection process of the new emperor. The most infamous was Cixi, the Empress Dowager of the late Qing, who effectively ruled China from 1861 to 1908, following the death of Emperor Xianfeng during the Second Opium War.

Great attention was placed on the appearance of women in the imperial court. Elite women would grow their fingernails to great lengths, showing they lived an entirely domestic lifestyle without manual labor. These were covered with elaborately decorated nail guards made of tortoise shells, gold, enamel, and precious gems. Clothing in general, and footwear in particular, were means by which female identity was framed in late imperial China. From at least the first millennium CE, elite Han women had their feet bound by tightly wrapping a bandage ten feet long and two inches wide around their feet, forcing the four small toes under the sole of the foot, until they eventually fused into a shorter and narrower stunted shape. Although criticized today, this highly complex process was a significant rite of passage for girls, having deeply symbolic association with domesticity, motherhood, skill at crafts, and eroticism. Whilst wearing finely embroidered "lotus shoes" over one's bound feet was practiced in Ming China, under Qing rule, Manchu women were forbidden from binding their feet.

Most attention is given to the illustrious lifestyles of the imperial family in the Forbidden City, but there were a great variety of other groups involved in the daily routines of life in the palace, whose stories are frequently relegated to the background. The Forbidden City was home to hundreds of governmental officials, eunuchs, and soldiers. Apart from the castrated eunuchs, no men were allowed in the Forbidden City during the hours of night, and were only admitted to the Outer Court, even during the day.

The governmental officials were in some sense political, cultural, and religious figures, all at the same time. They were civil officials and Confucian scholars, with their own institutions (Confucian temples in all the counties and prefectures, schools in some of them, an imperial academy at the capital). As local officials, they also had religious duties, performing sacrifices and offering prayers. However, their main role was to serve as institutional and intellectual staff for the effective management of the empire.

There were three levels that civil officials could hold in the imperial government, each having different proximities to the emperor's voice and ear: they could serve the monarch from the central compound of the Forbidden City; they could work in the Cabinet Hall located east of the Wumen Gate; or they worked in the lesser offices distributed around the southern and western parts of the Outer Court. It was via the Cabinet that the emperor transmitted orders to the various civil departments of the capital. Ministers working in each level resided in separate districts within the Forbidden City, demarcated from one another by high walls and gates.

As with other areas of the Forbidden Palace, the relationship between governmental ministers and the emperor changed under the Qing, as more affairs of state and ceremony were carried out within the Inner Court. Emperors, such as Kangxi, Yongzheng, and Qianlong, chose to surround themselves with advisors within their inner palaces. Many of these advisors were Manchu or Mongol, reflecting their mistrust of the Han staff of the capital.

Eunuchs were male servants that had been castrated at a young age, ensuring they could not father children (and spoil the imperial lineage). They did a wide range of domestic services, helped maintain the order of day-to-day affairs, and ensured the cleanliness of the palace. Eunuchs are frequently romanticized as being money-hungry, power-seeking individuals that surrounded the emperor and influenced the workings of the empire, and this may have been, to a large extent, true. Some have claimed that a decline in imperial and governmental power is marked by a relative increase in the power of eunuchs and the female members of the imperial household.

Three battalions of imperial guards made secure the confines of the Forbidden City, a total of approximately three thousand, five hundred troops. Soldiers manned the tall towers and walls surrounding the palace, escorted visitors at all times, and safeguarded the city at night. There was even a group of armed elephant riders that presented themselves each day outside of the Wumen Gate. During the Qing, only Mongol and Manchu soldiers were allowed to guard the Forbidden City, and only the latter were given positions close to the emperor.

Very few Europeans were granted access to the Forbidden City. The general view held by the Chinese during the Ming and Qing dynasties was that the Europeans were barbaric in nature, with strange habits, bizarre dress, suspicious gods, and bad manners. However, on rare occasions, envoys and visitors from foreign lands were granted access to join the emperor's presence, sometimes even for extended periods of time.

One of the most famous European visitors to the Forbidden City was Matteo Ricci (1552-1610), an Italian Jesuit priest, recognized today for his key role in creating a dialogue between China and Europe, despite his mixed success at converting the Chinese to Christianity. Ricci was educated at a Jesuit college in Italy before travelling to Portugal, India, and eventually China. His mission was to evangelize the population to Catholicism, which he carried out first in Macao and Guangzhou, before eventually making his way to Beijing. There, he managed to become the first European to gain access to the Ming dynasty court by gifting a clock to Emperor Wanli–a rare and exotic treasure in contemporary China.

During his time in China and in particular at the Forbidden City, Matteo Ricci immersed himself in Chinese culture and language. He became fluent in the Chinese language and well-read in Confucian and Buddhist literature. He first introduced himself to the Chinese elite as being a Buddhist monk from India in order to be more readily accepted. Despite these skills, his proselytizing mission promoting a different "Lord of Heaven" was largely unsuccessful. The empress dowager prayed to the image of the Virgin Mary and baby Jesus with the same language and rituals used in Buddhist practice, seeing them as being an alternative representation of the bodhisattva Guanyin. Ricci found Emperor Wanli more receptive to Western ideas of astronomy, mathematics, mapmaking, and science, than to religious thought. Ricci produced for the emperor a kunyu quantu ("map of the world") that depicts the known world in the late sixteenth and early seventeenth centuries. This is believed to have been the first European-style map published in China. Ricci left behind a vast body of textual records of his time in the Forbidden City, written in both Chinese and Italian. These provide scholars today with a unique, though undeniably Western, perspective into the inner-workings of the imperial palace.

A similarly accomplished Jesuit missionary was Ferdinand Verbiest (1623-1688). Born and raised in the Spanish Netherlands, Verbiest trained as an astronomer before being sent to Beijing to become an advisor to the Qing Emperor Kangxi. One other particularly famous foreign resident in the Forbidden City was Sir Reginald Johnson, a Scottish emissary from the British Empire in Beijing, who became the personal tutor of the young Emperor Xuantong in 1919. Much like Matteo Ricci, Johnson immersed himself in Chinese culture, becoming a proficient speaker of Chinese, and developing a keen understanding of how to engage in Chinese styles of diplomacy. He continued to be a close friend and advisor to Puyi after the emperor's abdication.

Chapter 4: Interiors and Activities

A 20th century depiction of the Chinese Imperial Throne

   The Forbidden City contains eight thousand, eight hundred and eighty six rooms, despite the popular narrative that states that there are nine thousand, nine hundred and ninety nine rooms in the complex. Each room had a different function; to list all of them in detail is beyond the scope of any single volume. Furthermore, the function of these spaces changed frequently over the centuries. Many had ceremonial uses, such as the Taihe Hall, which was used for imperial weddings and coronations. Textual records--such as those left behind by Matteo Ricci and the millions of records stored at the Qing dynasty archives–artefactual sources--including the hundreds of paintings produced during the Ming and Qing--and objects used by the imperial family and their staff, provide a body of source material through which we can get a glimpse into the private lives of those living in the Forbidden City.

There is, overall, a general lack in scholarly understanding of the precise practices taking place in individual rooms. However, by focusing on the three areas of art, food, and pastimes, and the material evidence associated with each, the ways in which values, beliefs, and identities were shaped by the use and production of material artefacts can be examined. This also reveals how interactions between China and the rest of the world were mediated by the travel of material objects, through the supply of food and through the collecting and connoisseurship of antiquities in particular.

The Forbidden City was a battlefield of power relations between government officials and their peers, and concubines against consorts and the empress. One figure's authority was unassailable, however: that of the emperor. The palace served as a space where his undeniable authority and wealth were visually promoted. Ornate imperial thrones were distributed around the Forbidden City, the most magnificent of which was found in the Taihe Hall. These uncomfortable seats of timber and red lacquer were wider and deeper than the human body, drawing the viewer's attention toward the seated figure.

This promotion of power was seen in particular through the art that was displayed within the rooms of the palace, used to show the might of the imperial rulers and the strength of their empire. Many Qing emperors had a keen interest in art, in particular that which showed their military might. They would frequently be painted by Chinese or European artists depicted on horseback, dressed in full military armor, or instead, using the bow and arrow in a hunting scene. Others commissioned paintings that commemorated significant events, such as Emperor Qianlong's victory against the Zunghars in 1755, illustrated by Jesuit artisans. Still others chose to portray themselves in religious scenes as bodhisattvas, according to Tibetan styles. Emperor Yongzheng produced one particularly fine set of thirteen portraits in which each image depicts the ruler in a different costume and fantastic setting. Emperor Qianlong is most renowned for his artistic interests, commanding portraits be painted of him right up to the final years of his reign.

Prestige was also reinforced by food and drink consumed within the imperial household. The Forbidden City had enormous kitchens of more than four hundred chefs, from which meals for the thousands of people that lived and worked in the complex were prepared. The emperor could choose from a staggering variety of dishes, and would be frequently offered large banquets served on the finest blue and white porcelain dishes, decorated with dragons that came from the Jingdezhen imperial workshops (modern day Jiangxi province). However, on a daily basis, many emperors chose to eat quite simple and plain meals.

The Imperial Household Department oversaw the supply of meals within the Forbidden City. They operated a number of specialized departments, such as the Imperial Buttery, which supplied tea and milk, and the Court of Banqueting, which managed state banquets. Under the

Qing, a great fusion of culinary styles were practiced as Manchu cooks worked alongside those invited from Suzhou and Hangzhou. The chefs of the Forbidden City held their privileged positions for life, and their sons were allowed to inherit their roles.

The ingredients required for this conspicuous consumption came from across the empire, and even beyond. Much was bought directly from the markets of Beijing, and imperial farming estates in the capital's hinterland supplied grains, fruit, vegetables, and meat. More exotic ingredients that could not be grown in the cold, northern climate were gathered as tribute from each province. Such exchanges were frequently described within a discourse of gift-giving and bribery. These included different types of melons, aubergines, cucumbers, apricots, peaches, and honey. The best quality rice came from the emperor's own paddies in Yuquan, Fengzeyuan, and Tangquan, and was even imported from the mountains of Korea. The Imperial Buttery was supplied by dairy farms at Zhangjiakou, on the other side of the Great Wall of China.

The literati, or scholarly gentlemen, of late imperial China developed a strong culture of collecting and connoisseurship, based on changeable ideals of "good taste." The Qing emperors made ample use of their tremendous wealth to collect ancient artefacts, works of art by acclaimed painters, and calligraphic texts of prose and poetry. Inheritance played a large role in this process, as unique objects and works of art would often remain within the imperial family network.

Some of these objects were quite peculiar: crickets kept in cages for fighting were very popular amongst the young emperors. Gongshi–otherwise known as spirit stones, strange stones, or scholar's rocks–were acquired from everywhere in the country to be added to the imperial gardens. These rocks serve as an ideal avenue into the complicated nature of the literati obsession with collecting. A flourishing genre of poetry and prose that classifies and discusses the merits of different rocks, and a vast amount of artwork, calligraphic poetry, prose, illustrated catalogues, and instructional manuals were produced linked to gongshi in general during the Ming, and frequently to individually named rocks. This heritage provided these rocks and their owners with cultural prestige. From the 16th century there was an increasing interest in the geography of where a thing was made, and "famous products" (ming chan) from different parts of China. Thousands of these rocks traveled by ship along the rivers and canals of China, sent to Kaifeng from Suzhou and Dongting Lake in Hunan by the "Flower and Rock Network" of Emperor Huizong. These were carefully prepared to minimise damage to the stones by plugging the holes with mud and glue, which was later washed away. From about 1550 CE, Taihu rocks up to fifty feet high were being transported from Suzhou to be incorporated into "artificial mountains" in "southern-style" gardens at the Imperial Capital.

Of all collectors in the history of the Forbidden City, if not the capital or even the entire country, Emperor Qianlong was the most prolific collector during his lifetime. He collected everything: books, artwork, ancient bronzes and steles, works of calligraphy, seals, natural objects, and anything else he considered rare or tasteful. He was also a prolific writer, composing more than forty thousand poems with perfect calligraphy, stamped in red ink with a seal from his extensive collection. Qianlong also collected weaponry to emphasize his military might and Manchu heritage. Many of these were designed by the emperor himself, categorized by him as being either "Heavenly," "Earthly," or "Human."

The emperors of the Ming dynasty did not share the Qing obsession with collecting and connoisseurship. On the contrary, many Ming rulers depleted the rich collections of their ancestors–in particular those of the Tang and Song–by selling their treasures to pay their governmental staff.

The emperor's timetable was filled with a never-ending series of secular and celestial rituals and ceremonies, supervised by the Imperial Household Department. These ceremonies were drawn upon from a number of religious traditions: Daoism, Confucianism, and Buddhism, and during the Qing dynasty, the Manchu system of shamanist beliefs and ritual practices were integrated with those of the Ming. The emperor fulfilled his cosmic and corporeal obligations as the "Son of Heaven" through these rites and sacrifices, mediating between cosmological orders and the issues faced by his living subjects. Furthermore, the emperor had to exemplify traditional values, foremost of which was filial piety. Many rituals took place during the year in commemoration of the imperial ancestors. Without following this complex system of rites, the emperor risked losing heaven's blessing, which would bring disaster to his people.

Many of these ceremonies were directly focused on stages of the emperor's life, or significant events in the capital and state. These include the emperor's coronation, his birthday, declarations of official decrees, and the winter solstice. Other rituals held a more abstract and celestial function, focused on heavenly beings. The gods of the Earth, Sun, Moon, and agriculture were but a few of those worshiped in the Forbidden City, as it was through their pleasure that society remained safe. These services took place in the many temples located around the Forbidden City and Imperial City, such as the Temple of Ancestors and the Altar of Land and Grain. Buddhist temples, including those representing the Tibetan doctrine of Lamaism, were also established throughout the complex, decorated with statues, mandalas, and the eight auspicious symbols of Buddhism: the wheel, conch shell, parasol, banner, lotus flower, vase, two fish, and an endless knot.

A Ming dynasty blue and white porcelain vase with cloud and dragon designs, marked with the word "Longevity"

Music played a significant role in many of these events. Drums, chimes, bells, and a variety of other percussion instruments followed the emperor's movements, statements, and actions, chiming in a harmonious fashion to illustrate the cosmic harmony and order being provided by their ruler–indeed, the words "law" and "musical note" shared the same word. Emperor Qianlong had two particularly beautiful sets of twelve bells and chimes assembled in 1761, the former of bronze made according to ancient "bo" forms, and the latter of nephrite jade imported from Hetian.

Chapter 5: The Forbidden City in Modern Chinese History

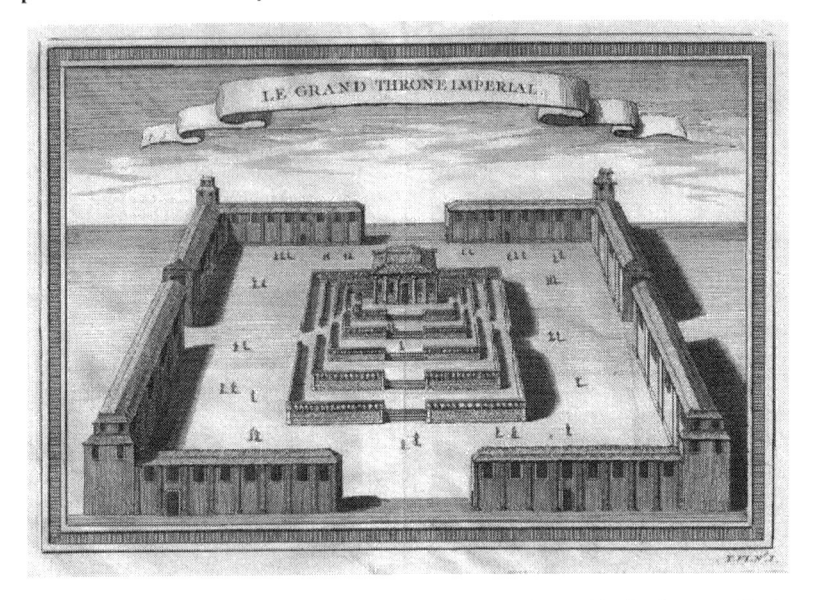

1756 Bellin View of the Grand Throne Room in the Forbidden City by Jacques-Nicolas Bellin

A gilded lion in front of the Palace of Tranquil Longevity

For centuries, opium was commonly used for its medicinal benefits, and mistakenly, as an aphrodisiac. Toward the later 19th century, the consumption of opium became more commercialized and enjoyed by a wider social spectrum. Opium spread from being a drug consumed by peasant labourers as a relief for physical exertion, to become a recreational activity conspicuously enjoyed by China's elite–including the emperor and his extended family.

Following a century of European mercantilist expeditions, the British East India Company acquired the opium-producing territories of India. Taking full advantage of this lucrative commodity, there was a sharp rise in the exportation of opium to China. Critics in Britain and America condemned the opium trade, and appealed to the principles of fair trade, diplomacy, and temperance. Protestant missionaries in China were also active in suppression campaigns against the opium trade. The Chinese emperors were appalled by the behaviour of the East India Company, and saw China as having a legitimate right to ban the opium trade.

Nevertheless, this trade culminated in the Opium Wars with Britain during the mid-nineteenth century, which caused irreparable harm to the country. In 1860, the Forbidden City was invaded by English and French soldiers, and during this tumultuous period, the Qing emperor Xianfeng died. The dowager empress Cixi fled, and subsequently regained a powerful position in the imperial court, though she massively mismanaged its finances and governance. A religious uprising in southern China, known as the Taiping Rebellion, occurred between 1850 and 1864, exacerbating the dynasty's downward spiral. On a broader scale, China was unable to keep up with other countries that were modernizing as part of the Industrial Revolution, such as the Japanese empire.

These events exposed a range of social and political problems that haunted the declining imperial system. The Qing emperors seemed quite unable to deal with either foreign or local threats, and to most of the population, it appeared as if the gods had withdrawn the Mandate of Heaven from the Qing household. This inspired the Boxer Rebellion in 1900. Organized by Yi Ho Tuan and supported by the Empress Dowager Cixi, this uprising was led by a secret society aimed at ridding the nation of foreigners and Chinese Christians. Thousands died during the rebellion, and though the rebellion failed to expel foreign influences, it provided the Chinese population with a renewed sense of nationalism.

There were increasing efforts for the Qing imperial regime to accept republican reforms, and in 1911, the Xinhai Revolution led to the abdication of the last Qing emperor, Xuantong (subsequently known as Puyi). Control of the country was transferred to the Chinese republicans, though Puyi made an agreement with them by which he could continue living in the Inner Court, whilst the Outer Court was opened to the public. In October, 1924, however, the Peking Coup occurred, led by General Feng Yu Xiang. Following this coup, in November, 1924, Puyi was forced to hand over the imperial seals stored in the Jiao Tai Dian, and to leave the Forbidden City.

A picture of Republican troops fighting to retake the Forbidden City on July 12, 1917, after Zhang Xun's attempted imperial restoration

In October, 1925, during a ceremony held at the Qianquin Gate, the Forbidden City officially became the Palace Museum, a public space in which the collections of art and artefacts gathered by the emperors were put on display. Nationalist China had mixed perspectives of the Forbidden Palace; Jing Hengyi of the Nationalist Government, then based in Nanjing, maintained that the museum ought to be abandoned, and its collection sold or distributed elsewhere, a motion that was passed by the Nationalist Government Council in June, 1928.

During the museum's earliest years they faced three main tasks. First was the continued publication of academic research based on their collections. Second was the exhibition of these collections to the public. The greatest issue that they faced, though, was the protection and transferal of the collections during the Japanese invasion. The Manchurian Incident took place on the 18th of September, 1931, in which Japanese soldiers detonated explosives on one of their own railways in Manchuria, blaming the attack on the Chinese, and setting a pretext for war. The armies of the Japanese Empire moved into north-eastern China, uncomfortably close to Beijing. Many thousands of crates carrying priceless cultural treasures were sent south across the country. Remarkably, not a single one of these boxes was lost in the number of years that this took place.

The entire collection, however, was not repatriated when peace was declared and the war ended. After abdicating, Puyi had taken measures to move some of the most valuable items of the palace collections to different locations. Many of these were never found again. Furthermore, when civil war broke out in China between the Communists and the Nationalists, a portion of the collection was taken by Chiang Kai-shek–leader of the Democratic KMT (Kuomintang) Party– to Taiwan in 1948. This is held today at the National Museum in Taipei. Yet another portion of the original Palace Museum collection is stored to this day in Nanjing Museum.

From 1949–the year in which the People's Republic of China was founded–communist political hegemony had terrible repercussions for the country's imperial heritage. Puyi had been treated as a puppet emperor of Manchukuo (Japanese-held Manchuria) from 1932 to 1945. However, under the Communists, he was sent to spend ten years in a Soviet prison. The last Chinese emperor died in 1967, in the midst of the Cultural Revolution that tore apart the country's historical remains. The Cultural Revolution was initiated by Chairman Mao Zedong, who urged students to destroy all ties to their imperial past. Many ancient buildings and historic artefacts were demolished, and hundreds of thousands of people were killed. However, despite the widespread vandalism and destruction across the country and the capital city, the Forbidden City itself remained largely untouched. This was thanks largely to the actions of Premier Zhou Enlai, who ensured the complex was guarded at all times.

Today, the portrait of Chairman Mao is placed conspicuously at the center of the Tiananmen Gate, facing Tiananmen Square, the central location of modern Chinese politics. He is flanked on either side by the political slogans: "Long Live the People's Republic of China," and "Long live the Great Unity of the World's Peoples." Indeed, Tiananmen Gate is seen across the country and the world, prominently featured in the national emblem of the People's Republic of China.

Although access to the sacred halls of the Forbidden City was denied to almost everyone for close to five hundred years, today it operates as a public museum, visited by thousands of people from around the country and globe each day. It is managed by the Palace Museum, maintained by the Department of Ancient Buildings, and protected by a number of Chinese heritage regulations, foremost of which is the Law on the Protection of Cultural Relics. More than one thousand three hundred people work there, half of which are devoted solely to research. The Chinese State provides approximately eighty million Yuan–close to ten million dollars–each year for the maintenance and continued operation of the complex. This does not include the revenue gathered from tourists. Over fourteen million people visit the Forbidden City each year, making it the most visited museum in the world.

The museum contains over one million works of art, close to two million artefacts, and millions of historical texts, stored in the Imperial Library. This surpasses the size of the Louvre museum in Paris by almost four times. To make up for the depleted collection following the Japanese invasion and Chinese Civil War, the Palace Museum has augmented the remaining treasures with objects borrowed or bought from other museums around the country. The current collection consists of painted art, porcelain, and other ceramics, sculptures, fine ceremonial bronzeware, enameled objects, jade, and assorted literati curiosities, dating from as early as the Qin and Tang dynasties. Many of the artefacts are unique, having been directly commissioned by the emperors, and carefully collected and preserved after their deaths. Others were gathered through conquest and tribute, collected as a hobby, or purchased directly from various parts of the country, and from foreign lands, near and far. Of particular note is the museum's remarkable collection of more than one thousand clocks and watches from the eighteenth and nineteenth centuries. The Qing emperors had an exceptional interest in timepieces, first collecting them from visiting Europeans, and eventually producing their own from workshops within the Imperial City. Many of these were made within the Forbidden Palace, but others were imported from the Americas, Japan, the United Kingdom, and Switzerland.

The Forbidden City is also a World Heritage site, listed by UNESCO in 1987. According to the nomination criteria, the site's universal cultural value is primarily architectural, coming from its uniquely large collection of well-preserved timber structures, the largest of such in the world. It is described as being the "best-preserved palace complex not only in China but also in the rest of the world" and representative of a uniquely advanced architectural character. Finally, the assortment of Ming and Qing treasures it contains is the largest collection of Chinese cultural relics in the world, making it a site of national and international importance as a repository of China's past.

Chapter 6: Conclusion

The Forbidden City is a uniquely important site in contemporary China. It has been featured in numerous films, the most famous of which is Bernardo Bertolucci's 1987 biographical film, The Last Emperor, which describes the life of Puyi (this was the first movie to have ever been shot at the Forbidden City). The museum has undergone much restoration since its listing. As such, the palace remains in an excellent state of preservation, seemingly frozen in time as the site would have looked in 1912. Tourism has played a large role in helping to develop a heritage industry for the generation of income. "World Heritage" has become a global and marketable brand that attracts tourists and investors who contribute to the local and national economies.

However, the Forbidden City also faces a number of very serious human and environmental threats. Beijing's atmospheric pollution is at an all-time high, contributing to the decay of the timber structures and delicate painted murals of the Forbidden Palace. Acid rain corrodes stone statues and the carved, marble balustrades have become stained by the smog that has settled across the capital. Furthermore, visitor numbers present a key threat to the site, with more than fourteen million people visiting each year. These are part of a process by which people and things become endangered and gain scarcity value, and by extension economic value. It seems to be that as soon as a "heritage asset" is noticed and defined in China, it is only a matter of time until it is commodified as an economic resource. Despite strict legislation regarding development in and around heritage sites, many commercial chains, such as Starbucks, have opened branches at the Forbidden Palace, which had led to fierce criticism.

Bathing Horses by Zhao Mengfu (1254–1322)

Equestrian painting of the Qianlong Emperor (r. 1735–1796) by Giuseppe Castiglione

Constant maintenance is therefore required. This is nothing new–indeed, one of the most popular legends surrounding the Forbidden City is that of Lu Ban, a semi-deified carpenter, believed to be the only one capable of reconstructing one of the corner towers of the city walls after it was demolished during the early Qing. However, even Lu Ban would not be able to provide a sustainable solution without drastic steps being taken in the near future. Without a management plan that offers a solution to these threats, our generation's children and grandchildren may only know the palatial site as the "Forgotten City."

Online Resources

Other books about China by Charles River Editors

Other titles about the Forbidden City on Amazon

Bibliography

Aisin-Gioro, Puyi (1964). From Emperor to citizen : the autobiography of Aisin-Gioro Pu Yi. Beijing: Foreign Language Press. ISBN 0-19-282099-0.

Huang, Ray (1981). 1587, A Year of No Significance: The Ming Dynasty in Decline. New Haven: Yale University Press. ISBN 0-300-02518-1.

Yang, Xiagui (2003). The Invisible Palace. Li, Shaobai (photography); Chen, Huang (translation). Beijing: Foreign Language Press. ISBN 7-119-03432-4.

Yu, Zhuoyun (1984). Palaces of the Forbidden City. New York: Viking. ISBN 0-670-53721-7.

Barmé, Geremie R (2008). The Forbidden City. Harvard University Press. 251 pages. ISBN 978-0-67402-779-4.

Cotterell, Arthur (2007). The Imperial Capitals of China – An Inside View of the Celestial Empire. London: Pimlico. 304 pages. ISBN 978-1-84595-009-5.

Ho; Bronson (2004). Splendors of China's Forbidden City. London: Merrell Publishers. ISBN 1-85894-258-6.

Free Books by Charles River Editors

We have brand new titles available for free most days of the week. To see which of our titles are currently free, click on this link.

Discounted Books by Charles River Editors

We have titles at a discount price of just 99 cents everyday. To see which of our titles are currently 99 cents, click on this link.

Made in the USA
Middletown, DE
22 July 2018